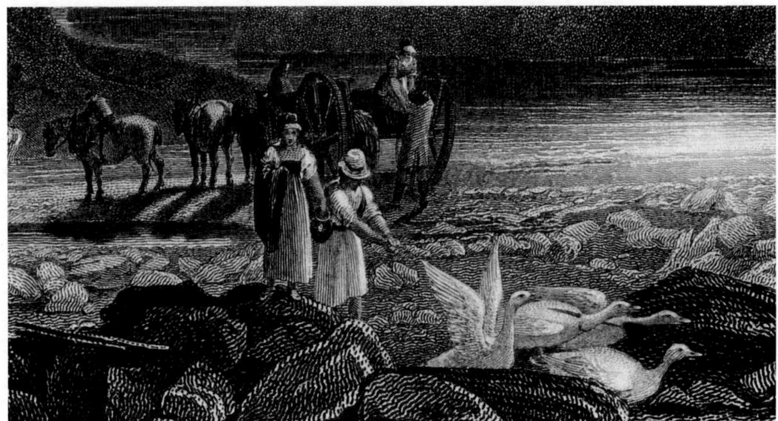

An History of Richmondshire

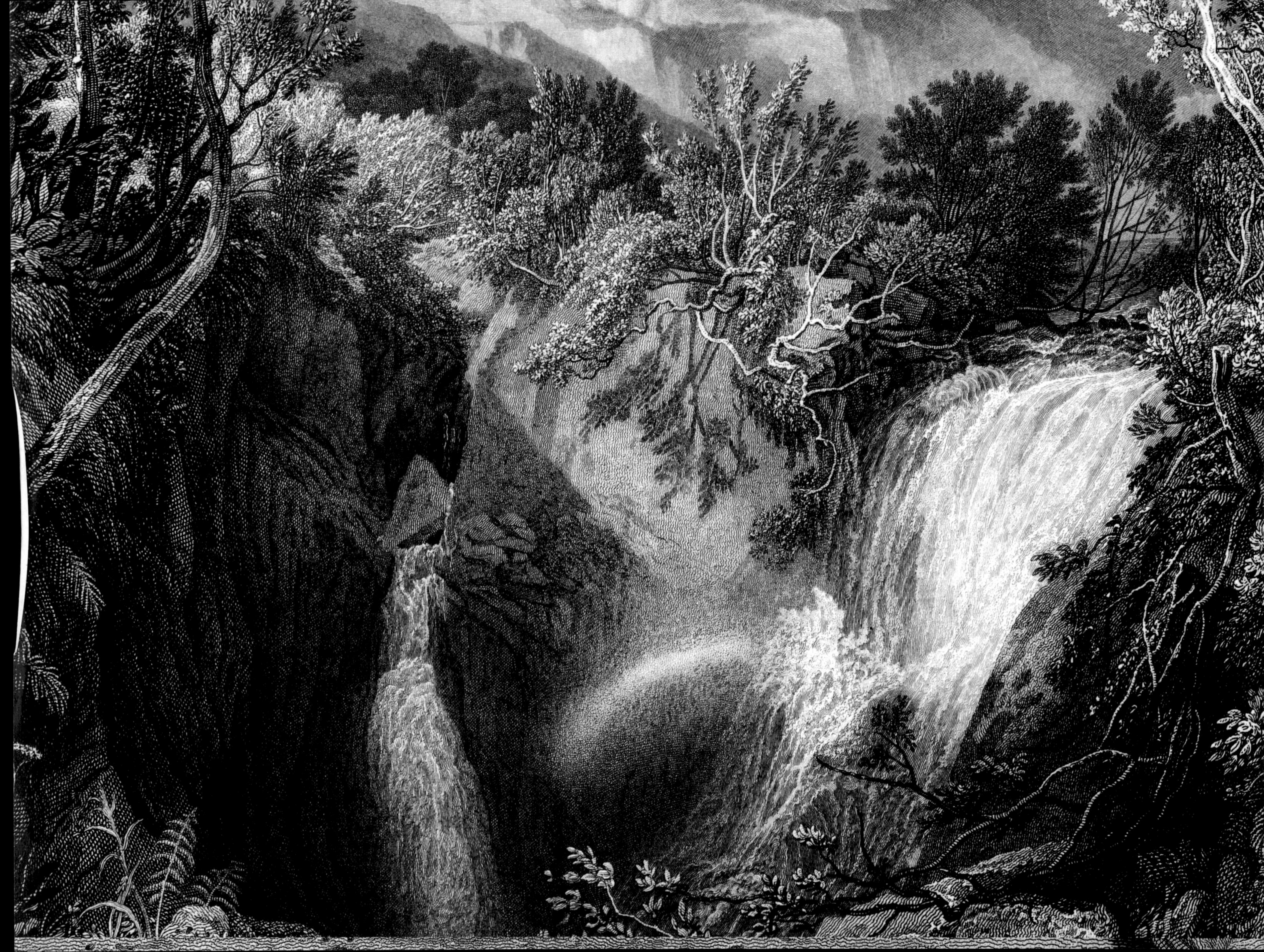

An History of Richmondshire

J. M. W. Turner

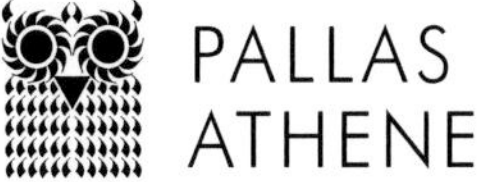

TABLE OF CONTENTS

1: RICHMOND, YORKSHIRE

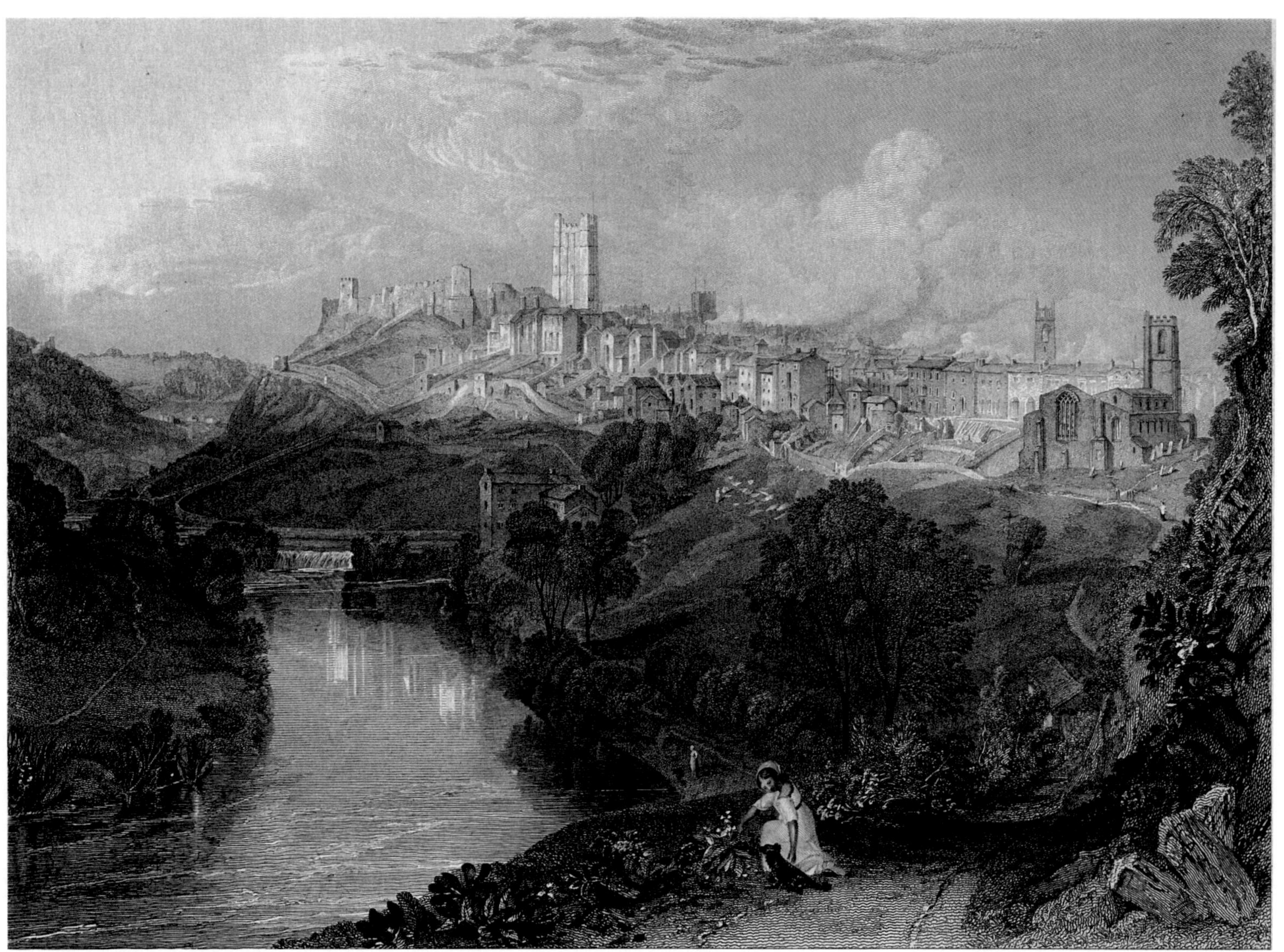

2: RICHMOND CASTLE AND TOWN

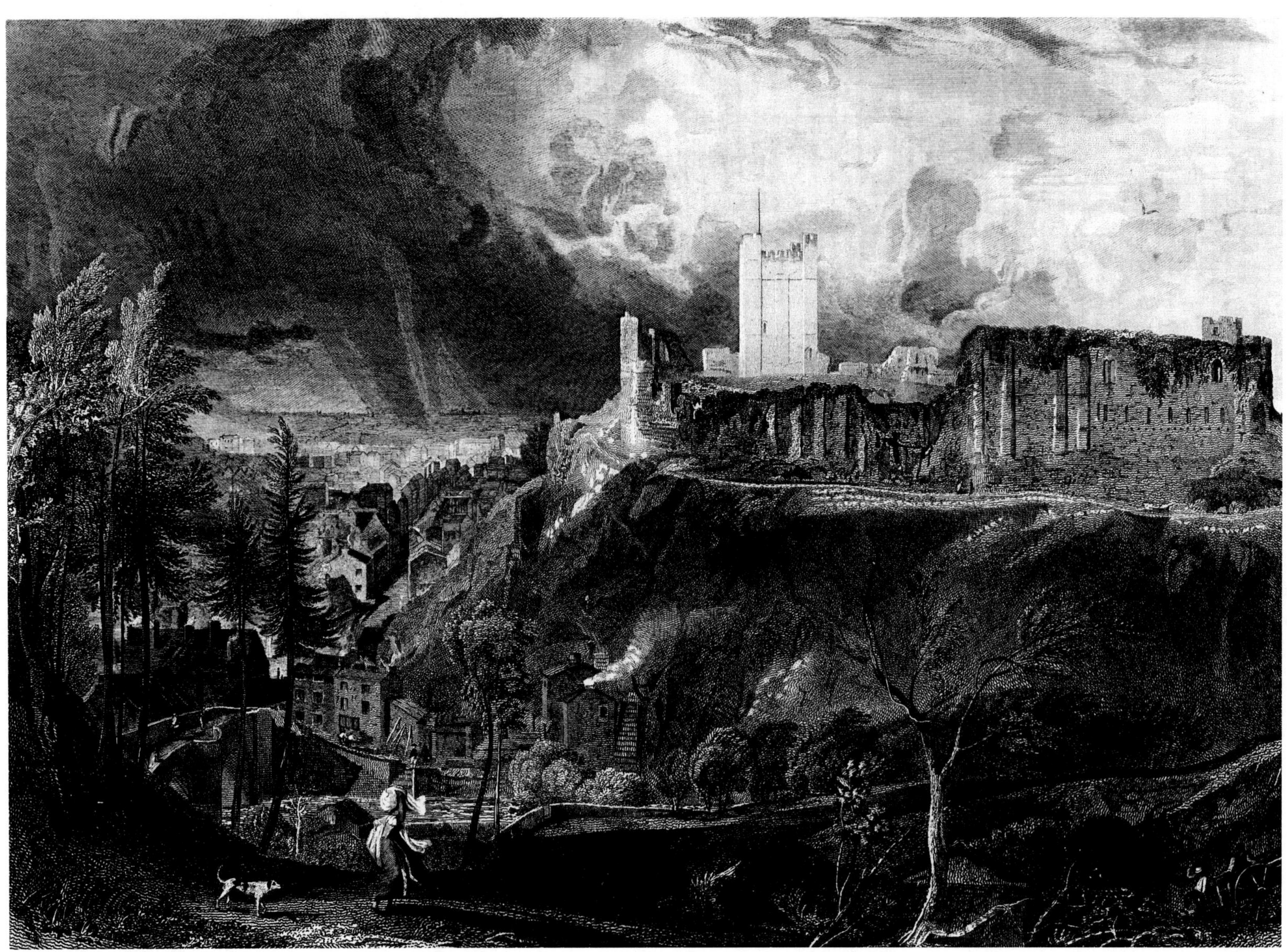

3: ST AGATHA'S ABBEY, EASBY

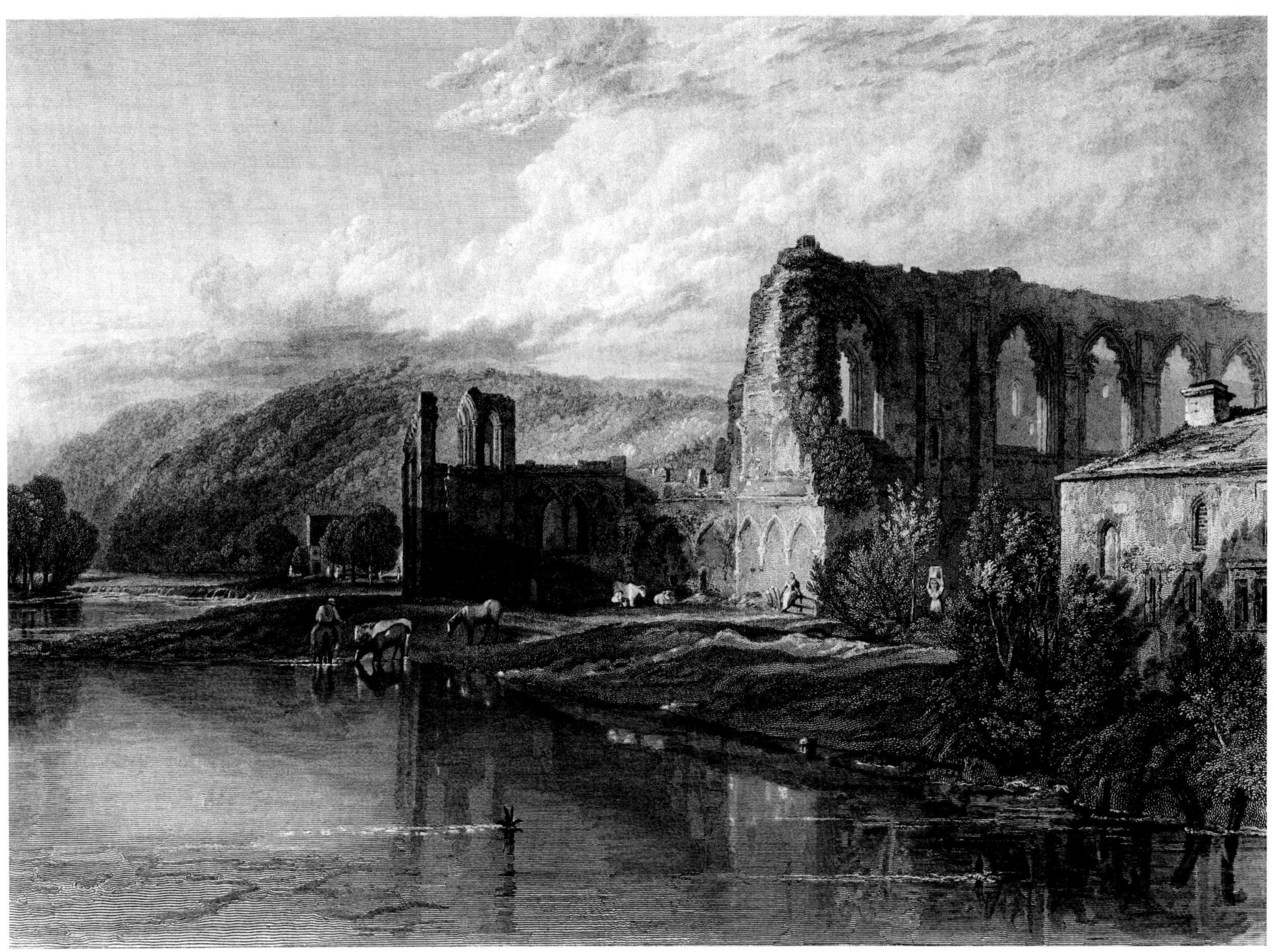

4: ASKE HALL, THE SEAT OF THE RIGHT HONBLE LORD DUNDAS

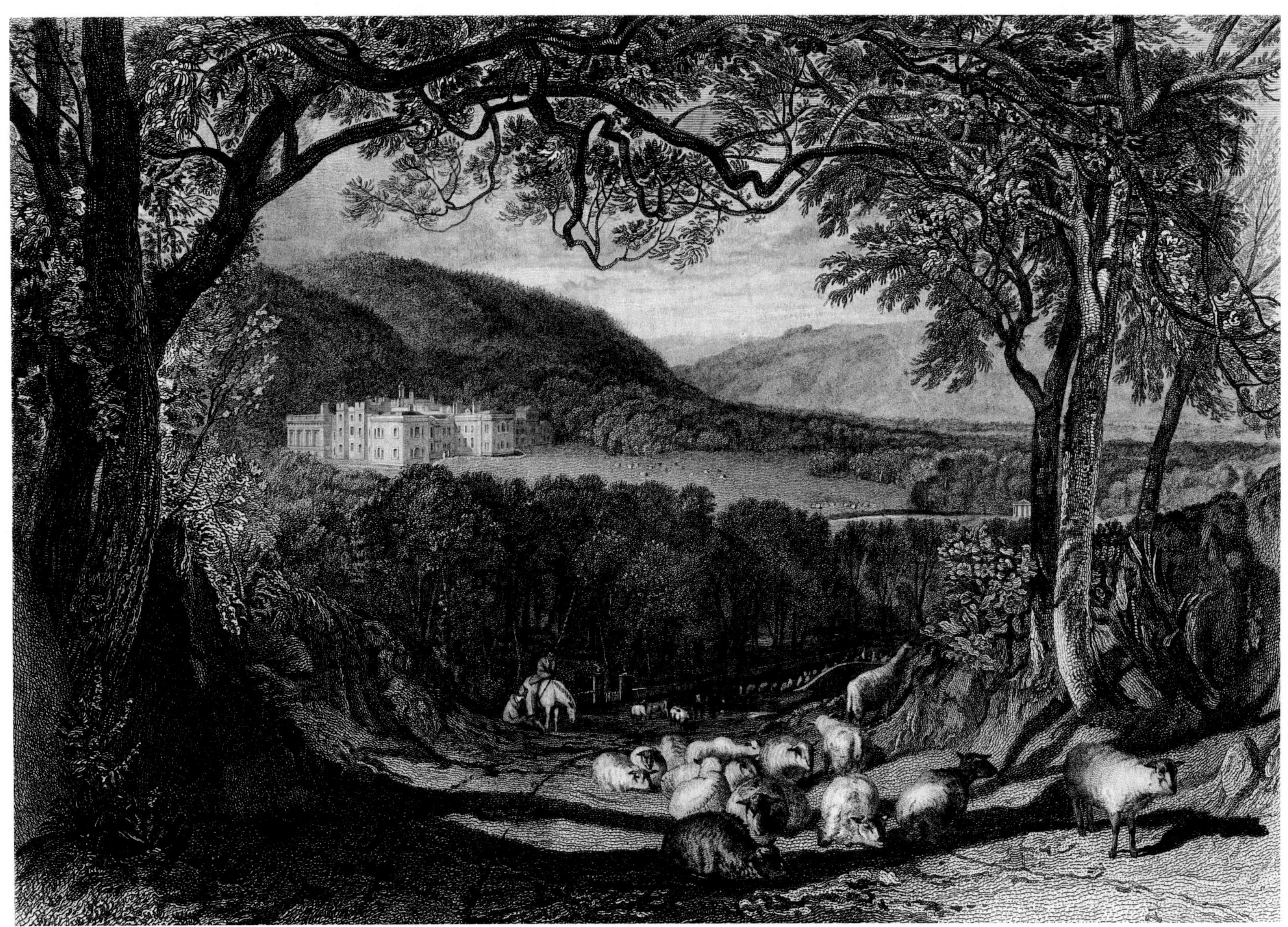

5: HIGH FORCE OR FALL OF TEES

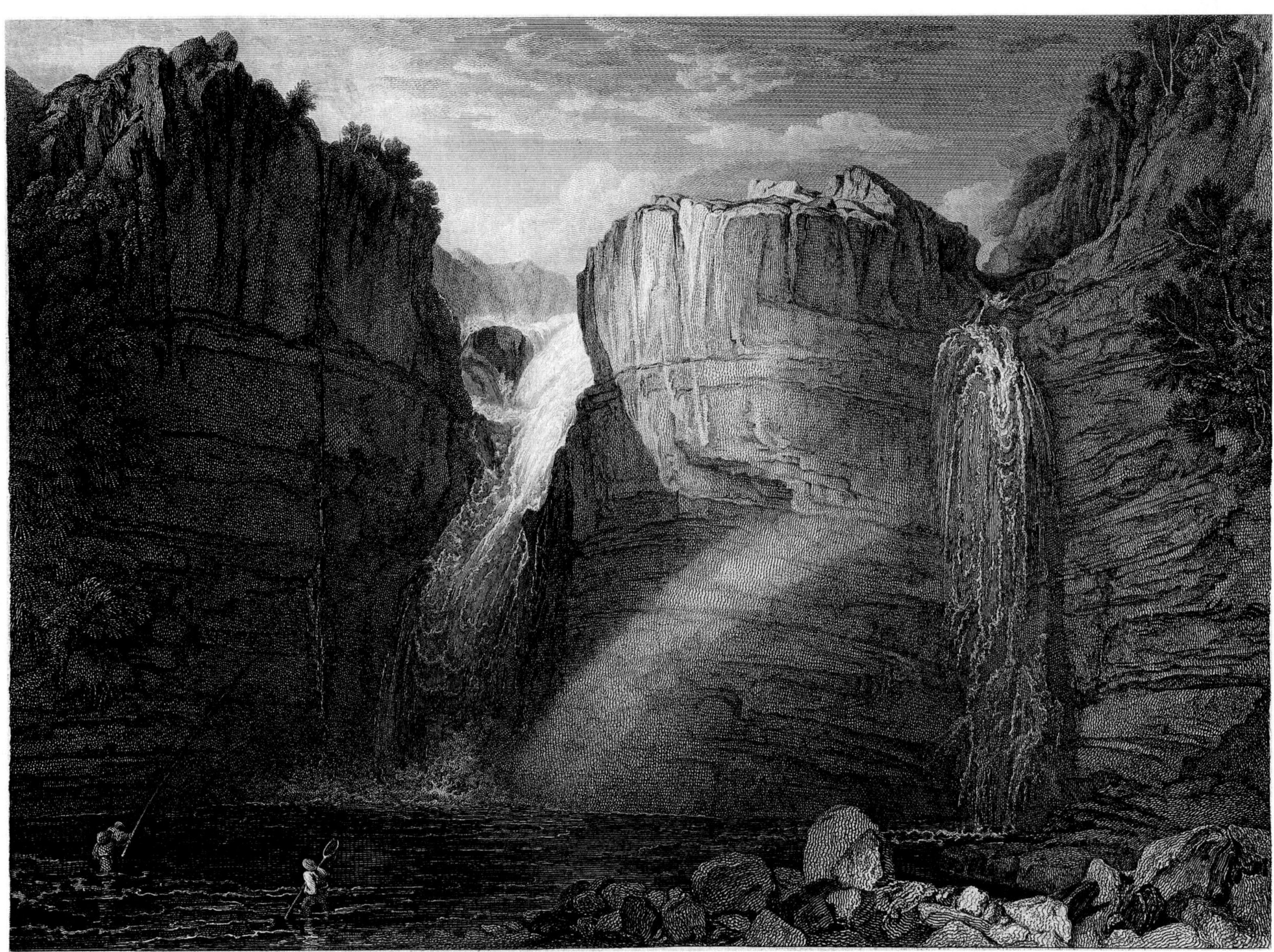

6: EGGLESTONE ABBEY, NEAR BARNARD CASTLE

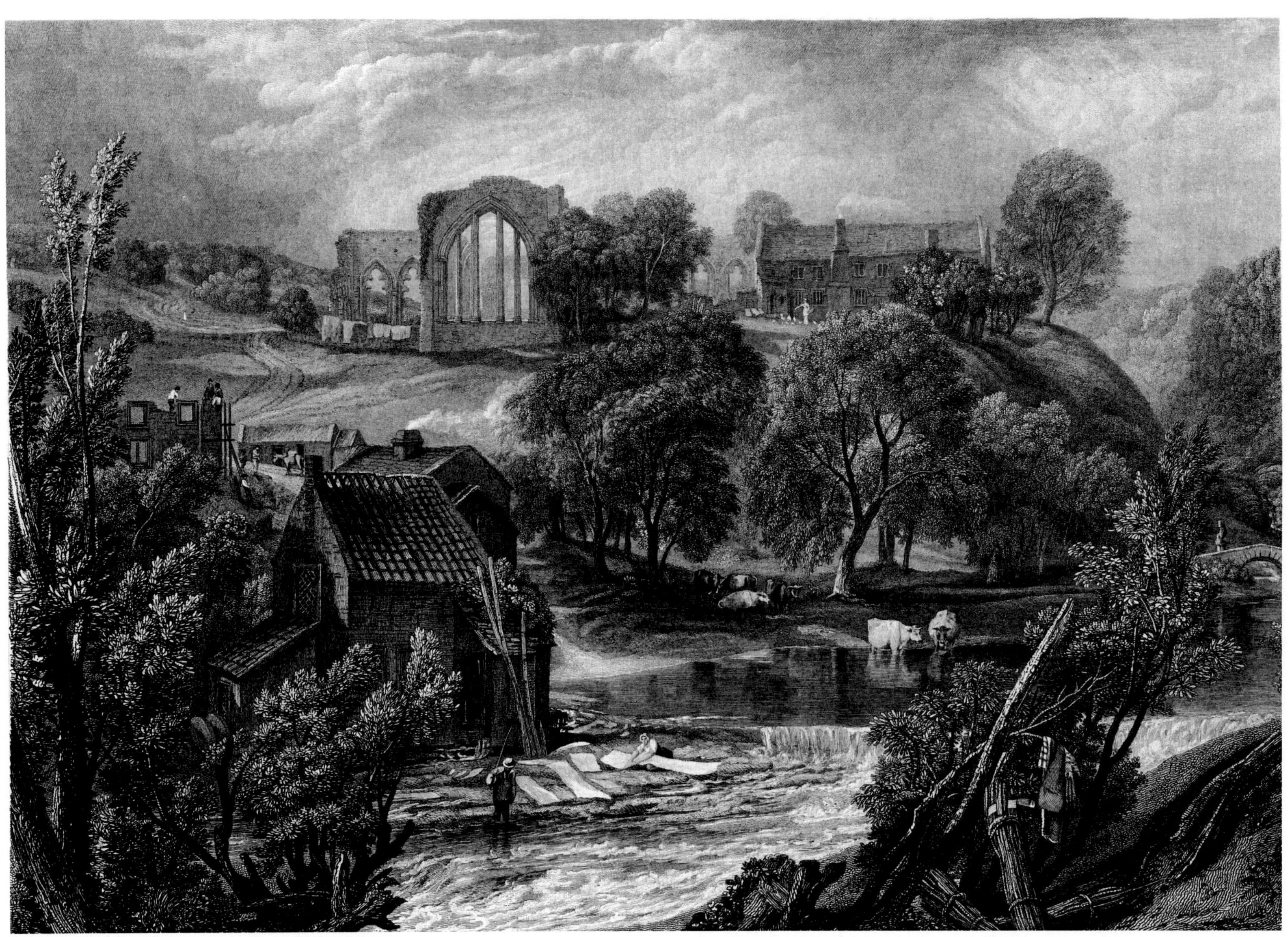

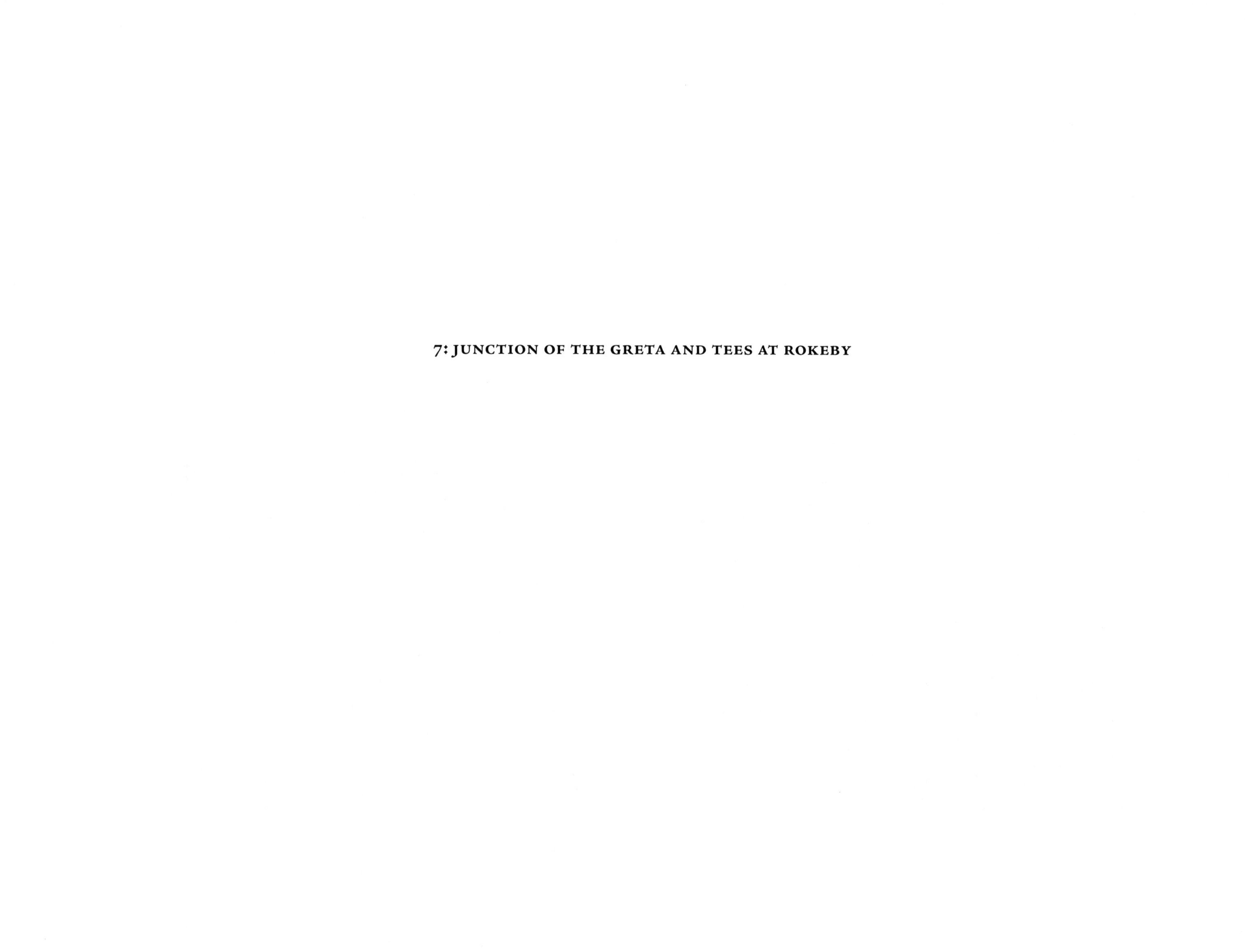

7: JUNCTION OF THE GRETA AND TEES AT ROKEBY

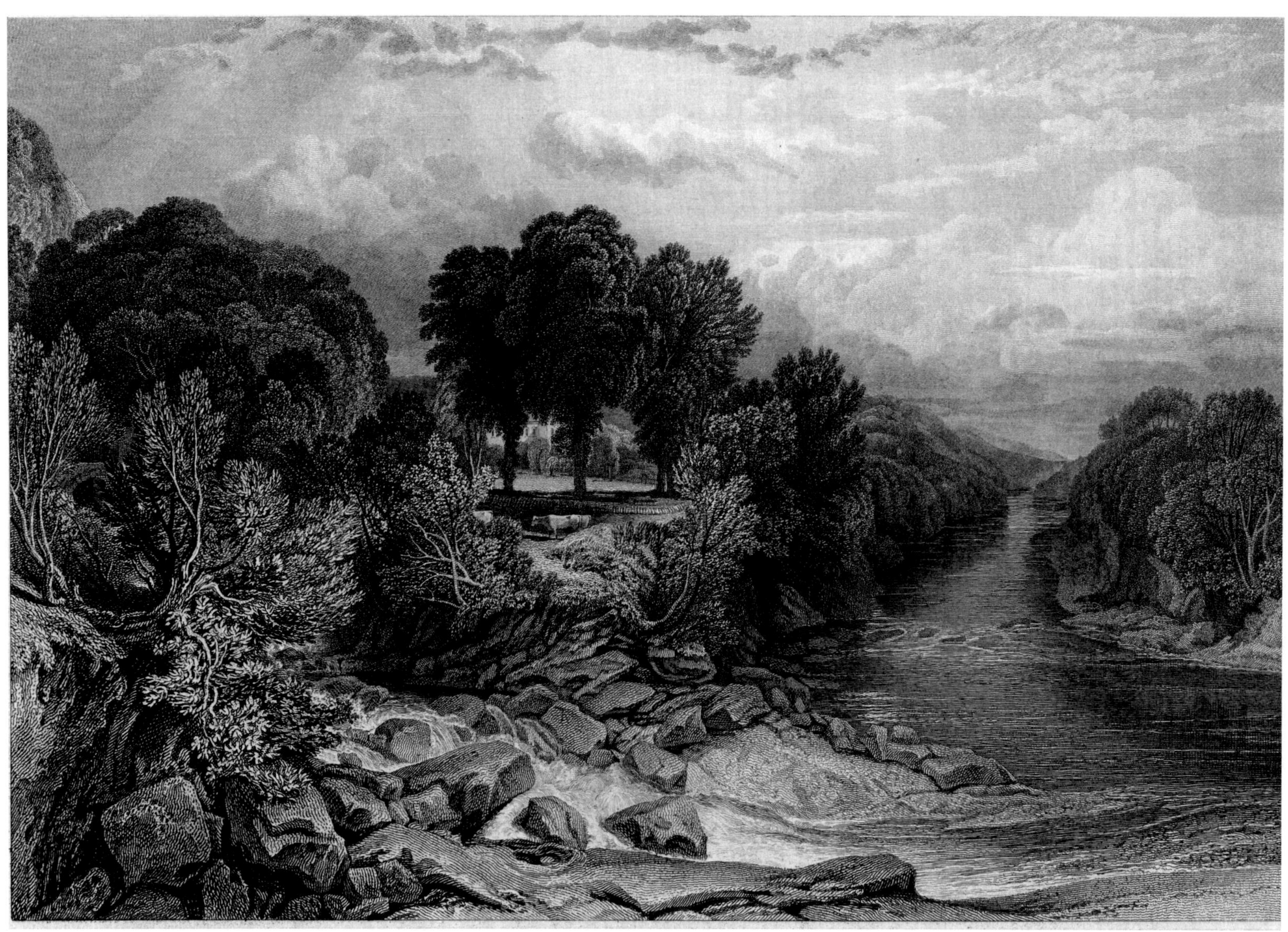

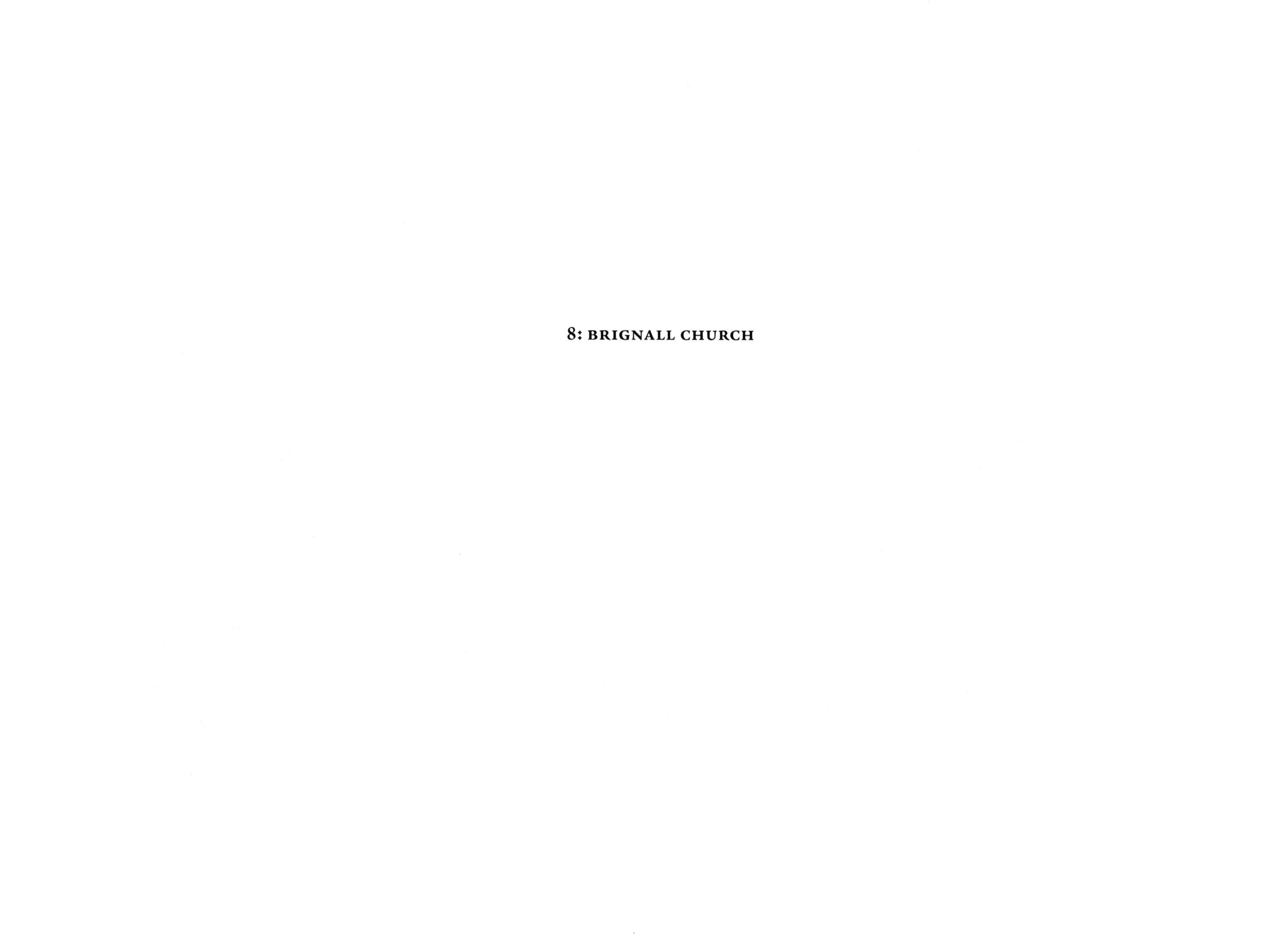

8: BRIGNALL CHURCH

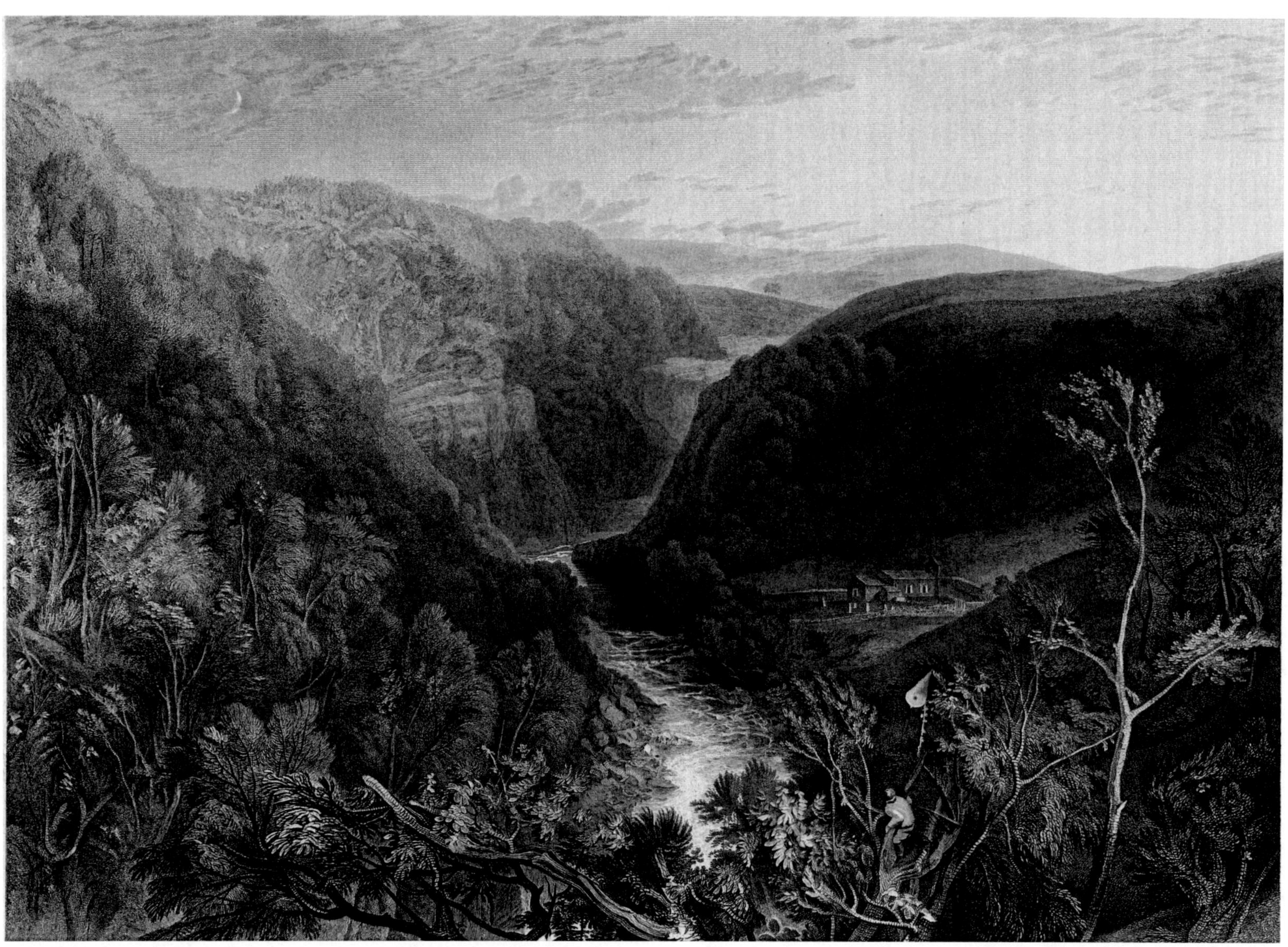

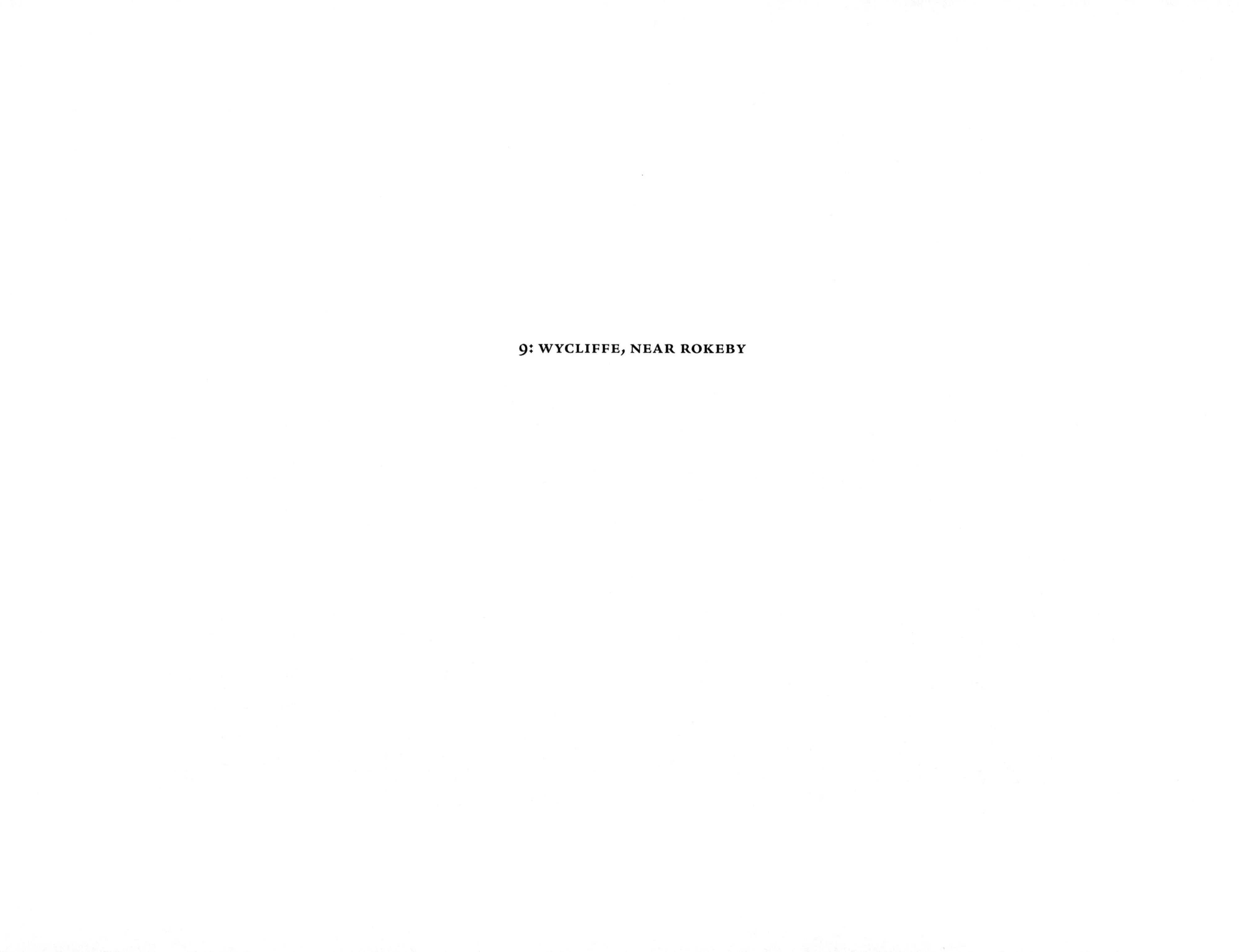

9: WYCLIFFE, NEAR ROKEBY

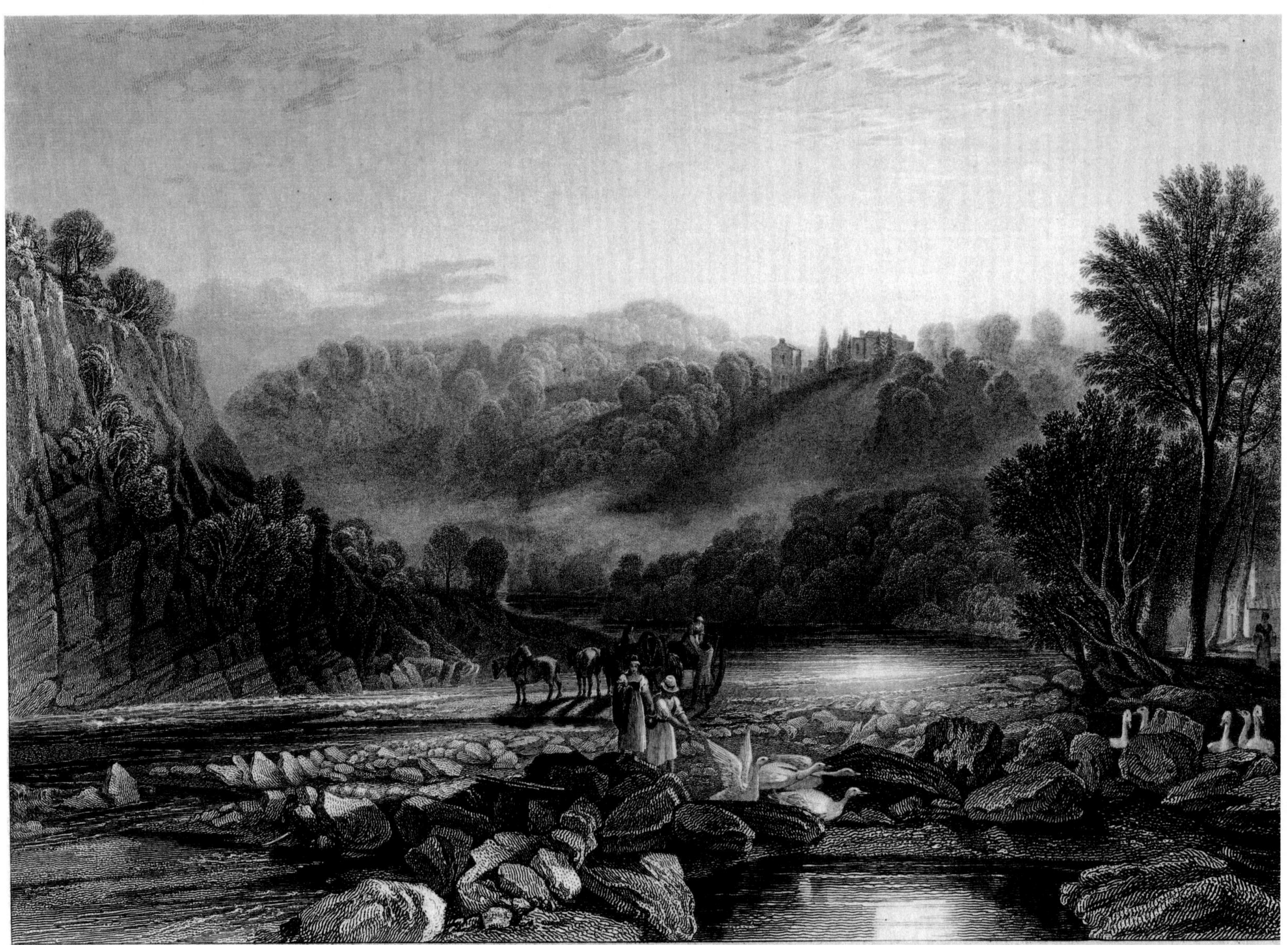

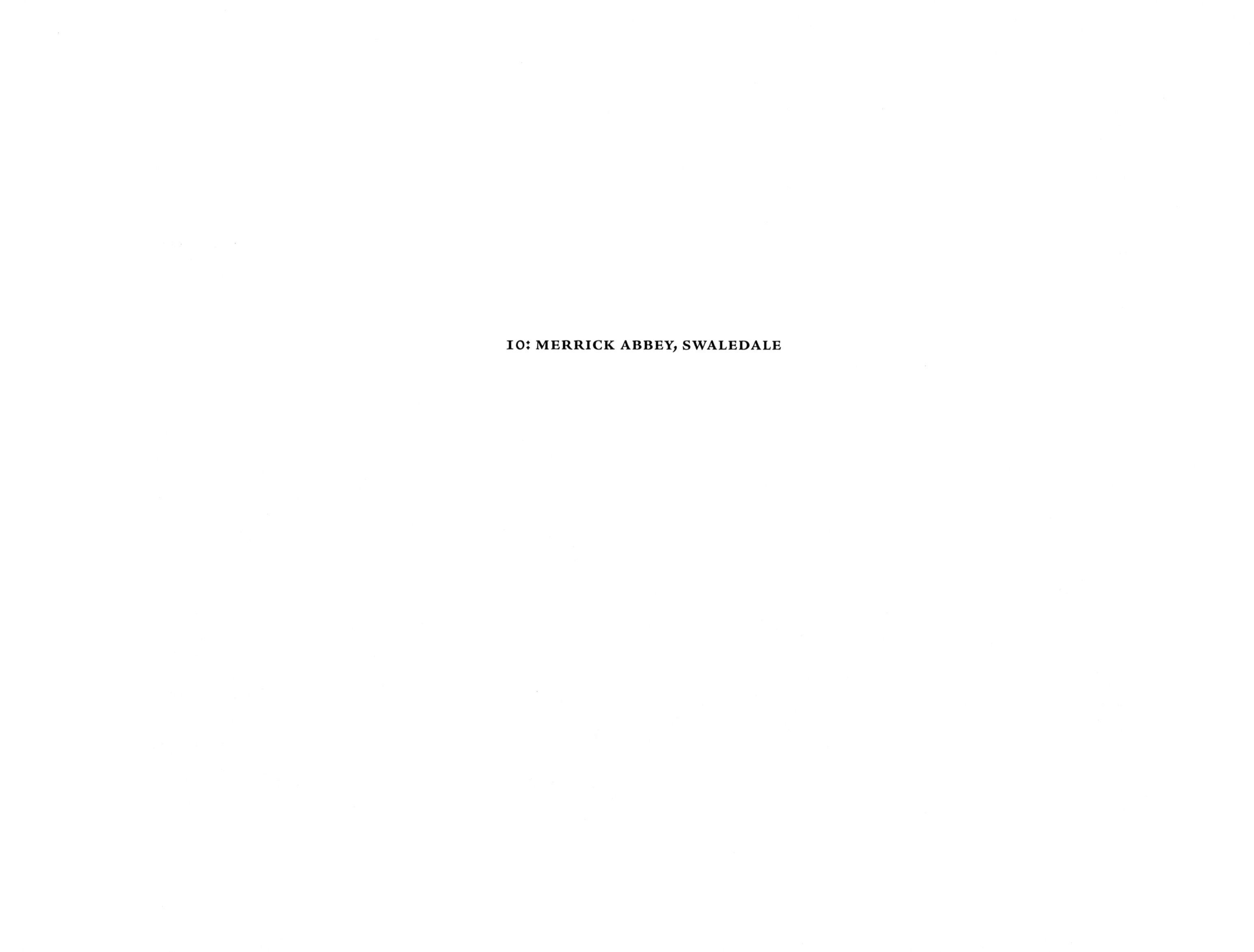

10: MERRICK ABBEY, SWALEDALE

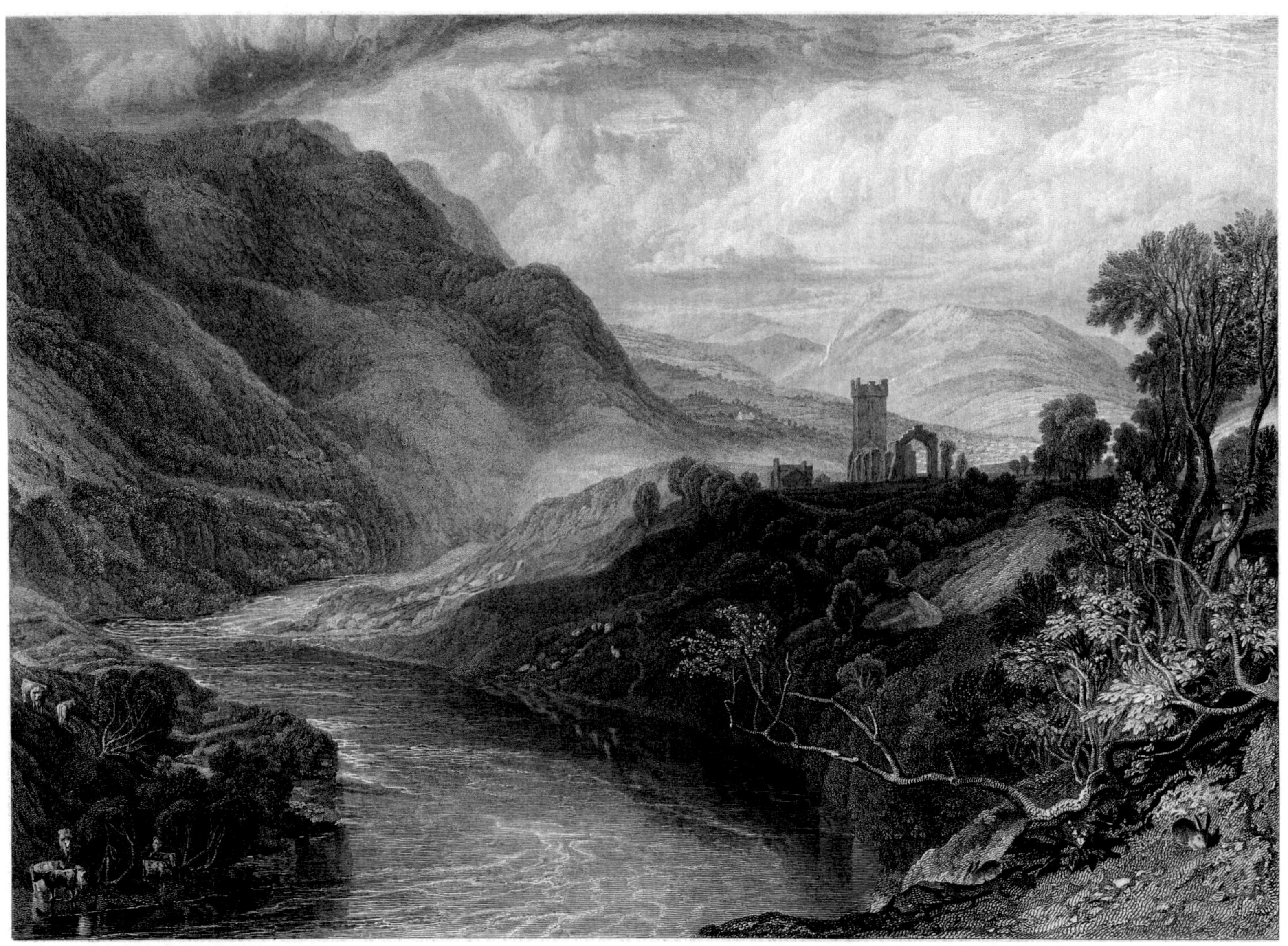

II: AYSGARTH FORCE

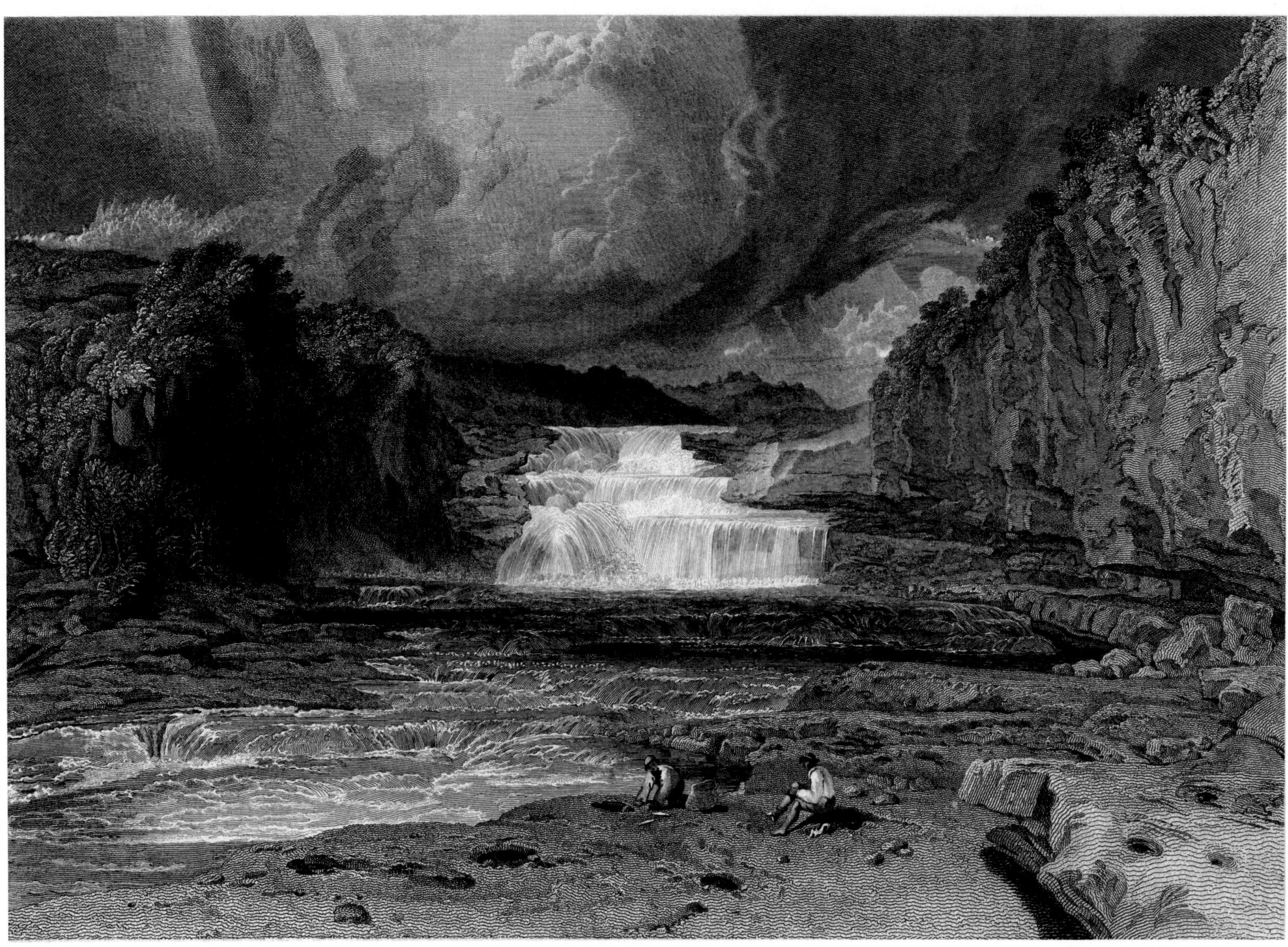

12: SIMMER LAKE, NEAR ASKRIG

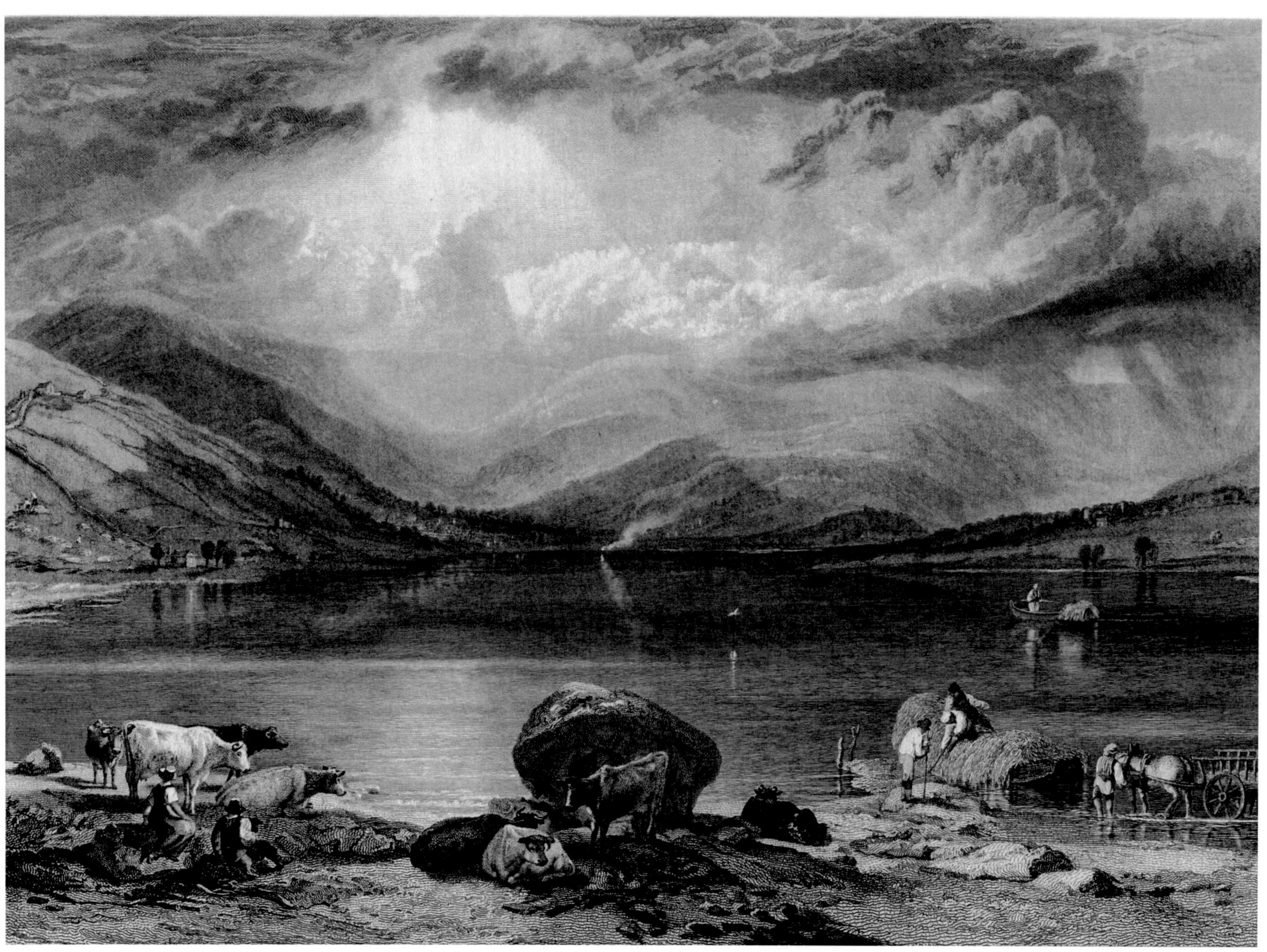

13: HARDRAW FALL

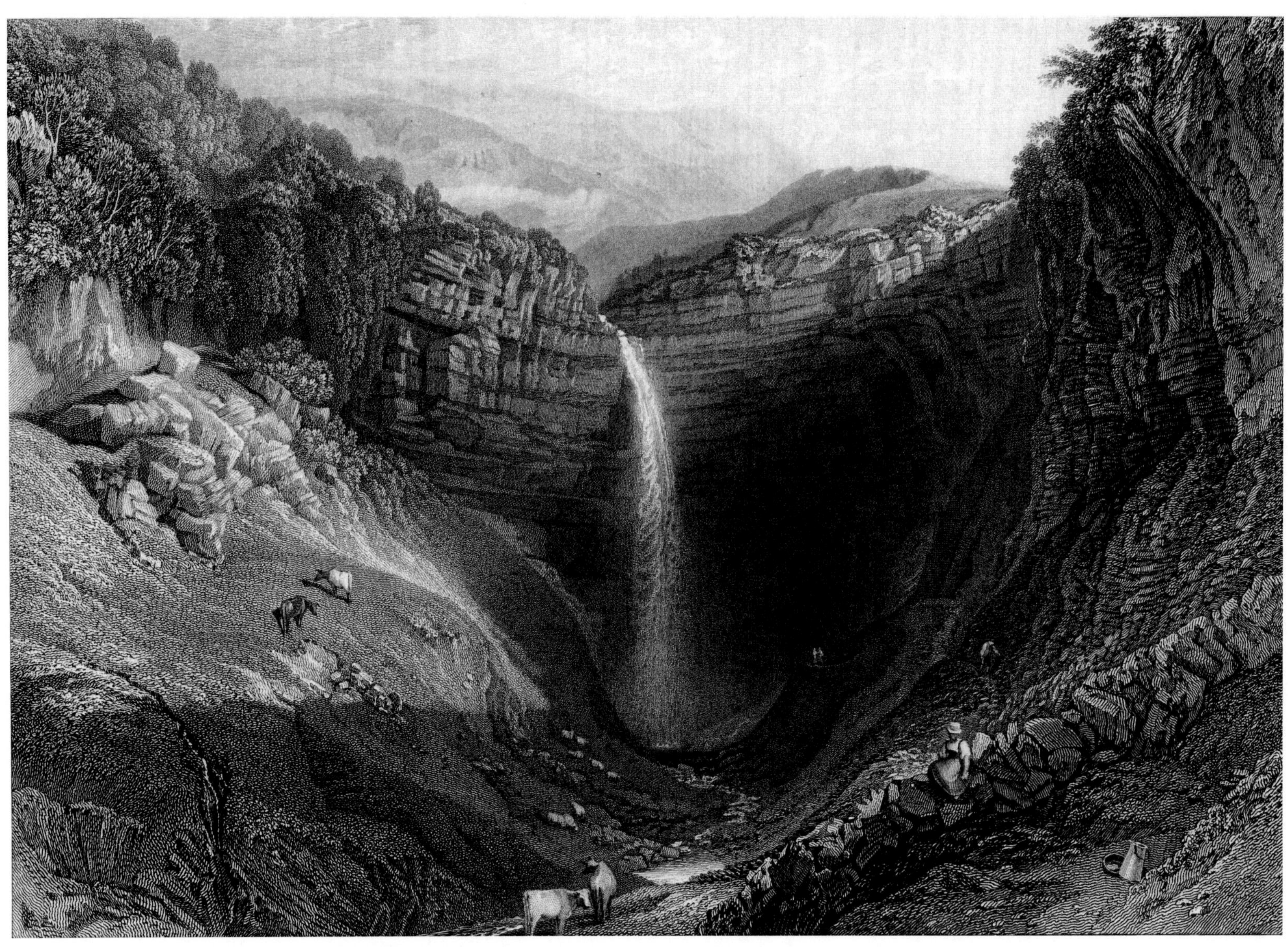

14: MOSS DALE FALL

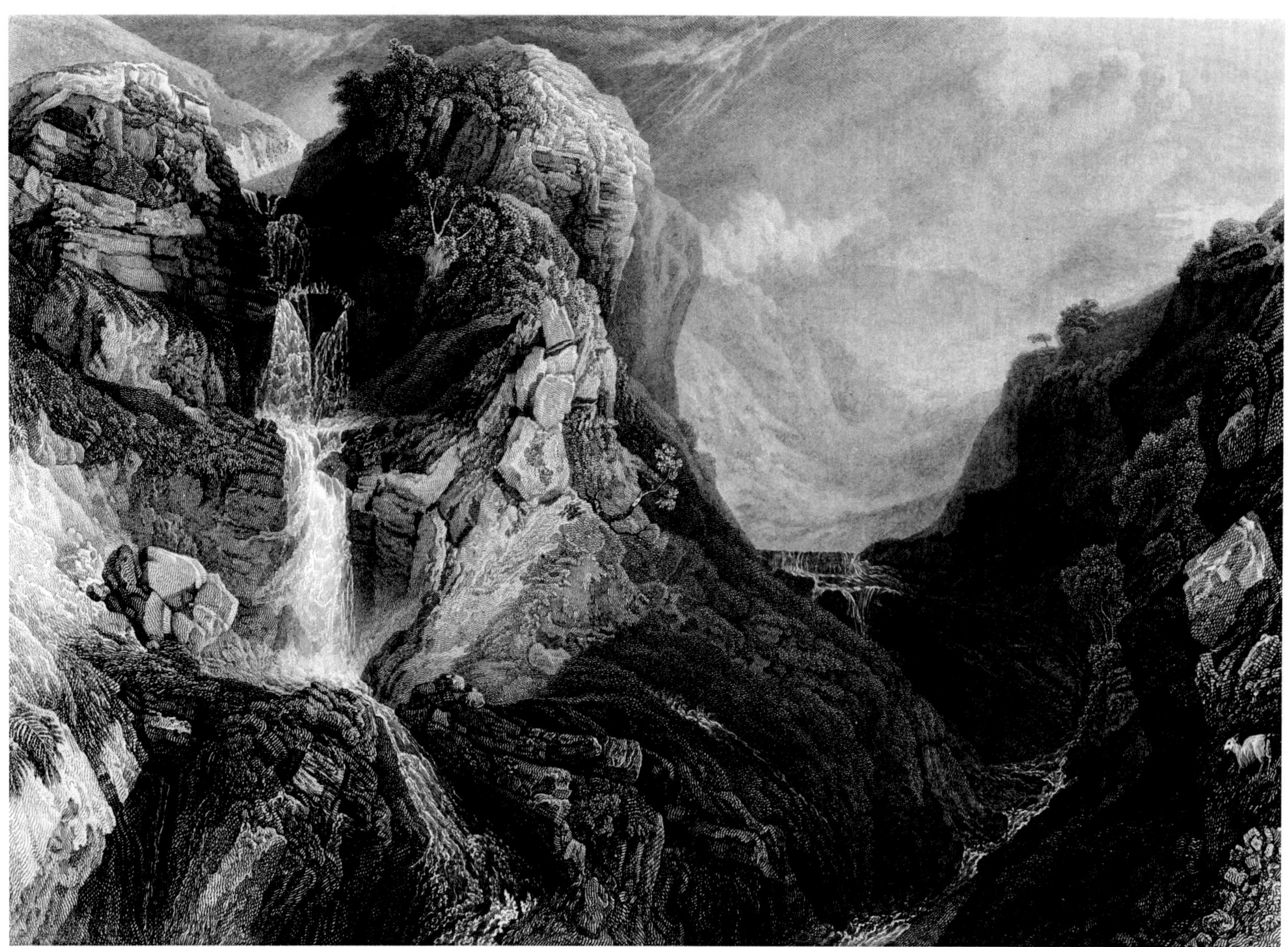

15: CROOK OF THE LUNE, LOOKING TOWARDS HORNBY CASTLE

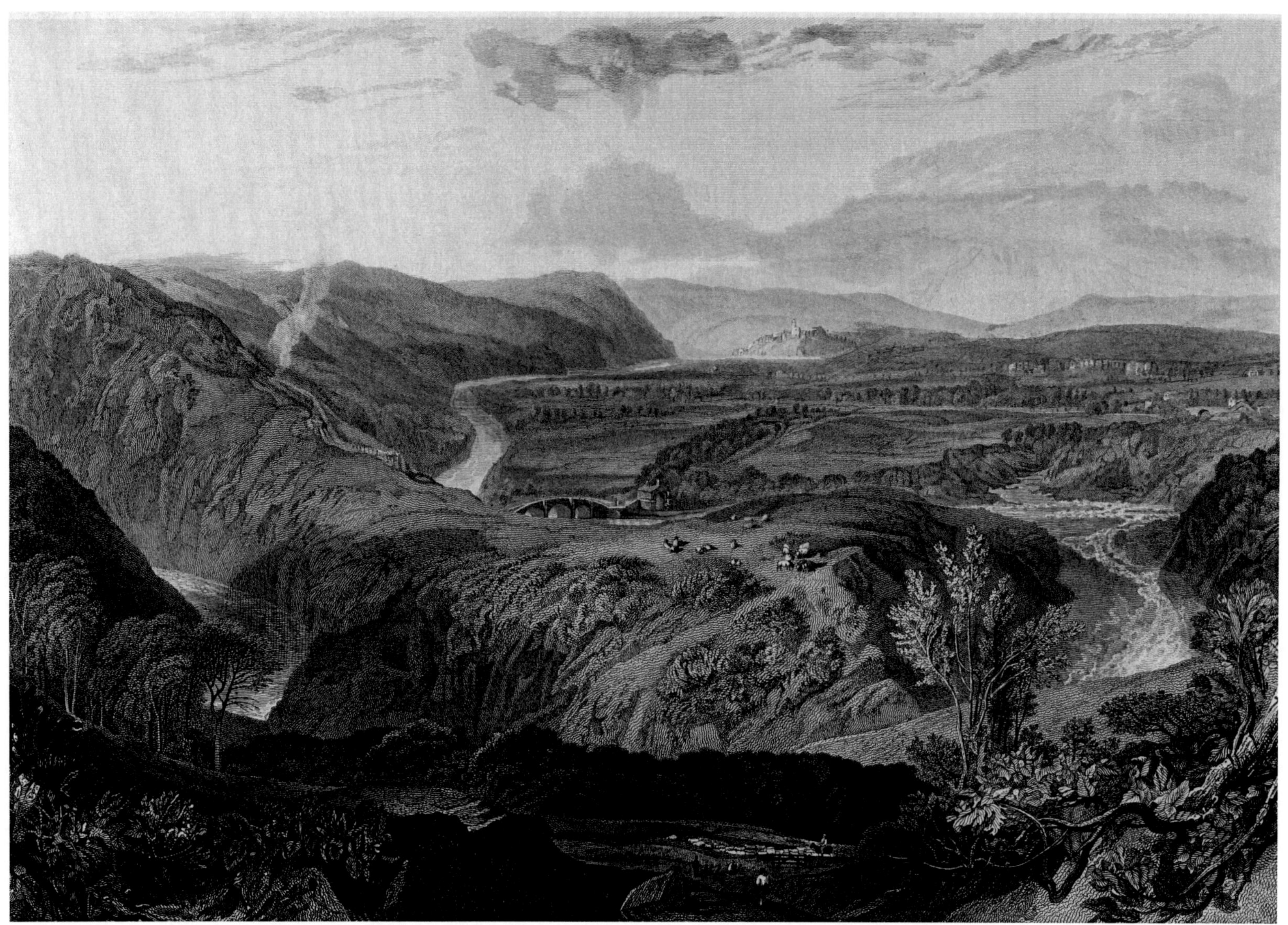

16: INGLEBOROUGH, FROM HORNBY CASTLE TERRACE

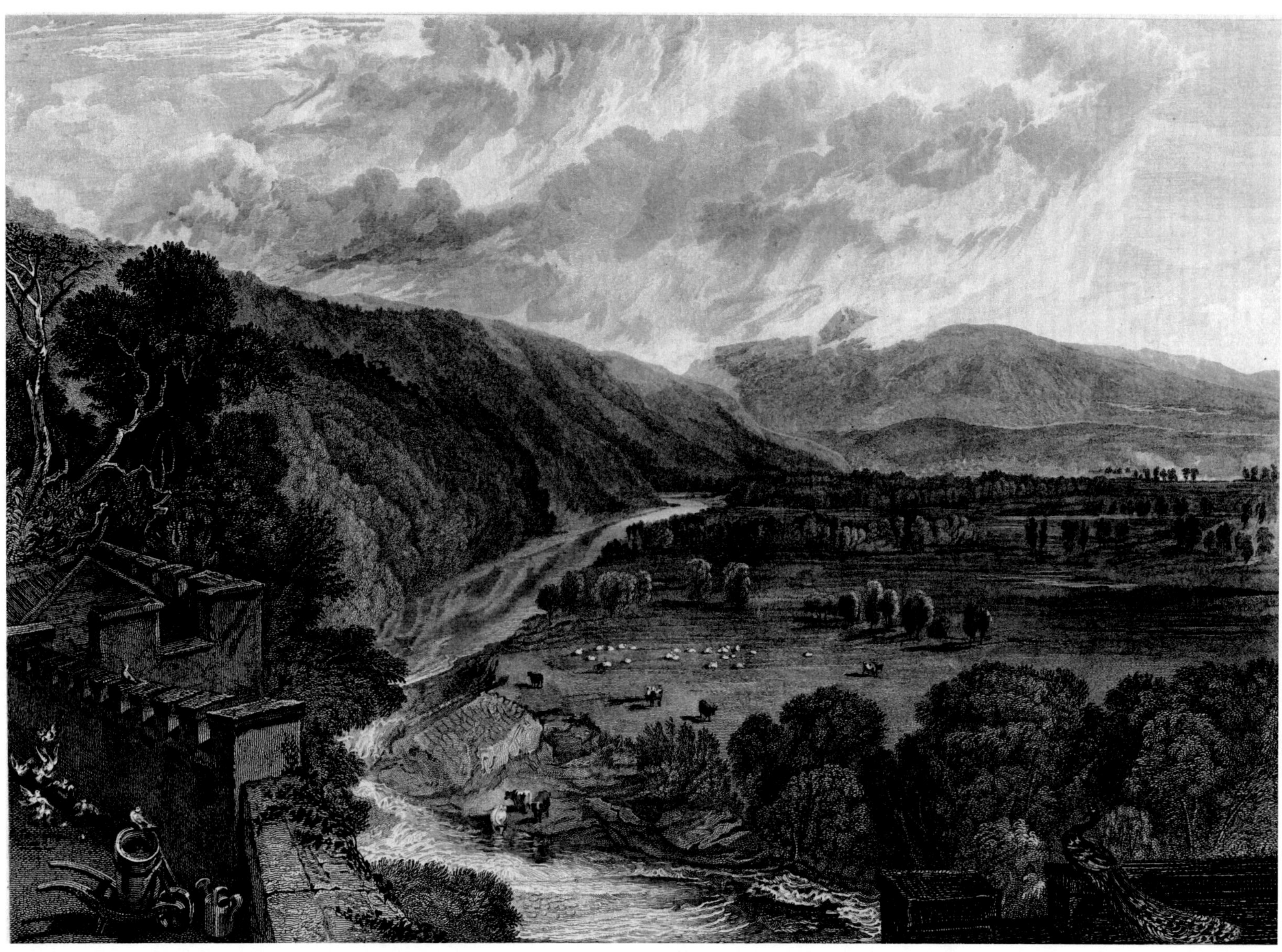

17: HORNBY CASTLE FROM TATHAM CHURCH

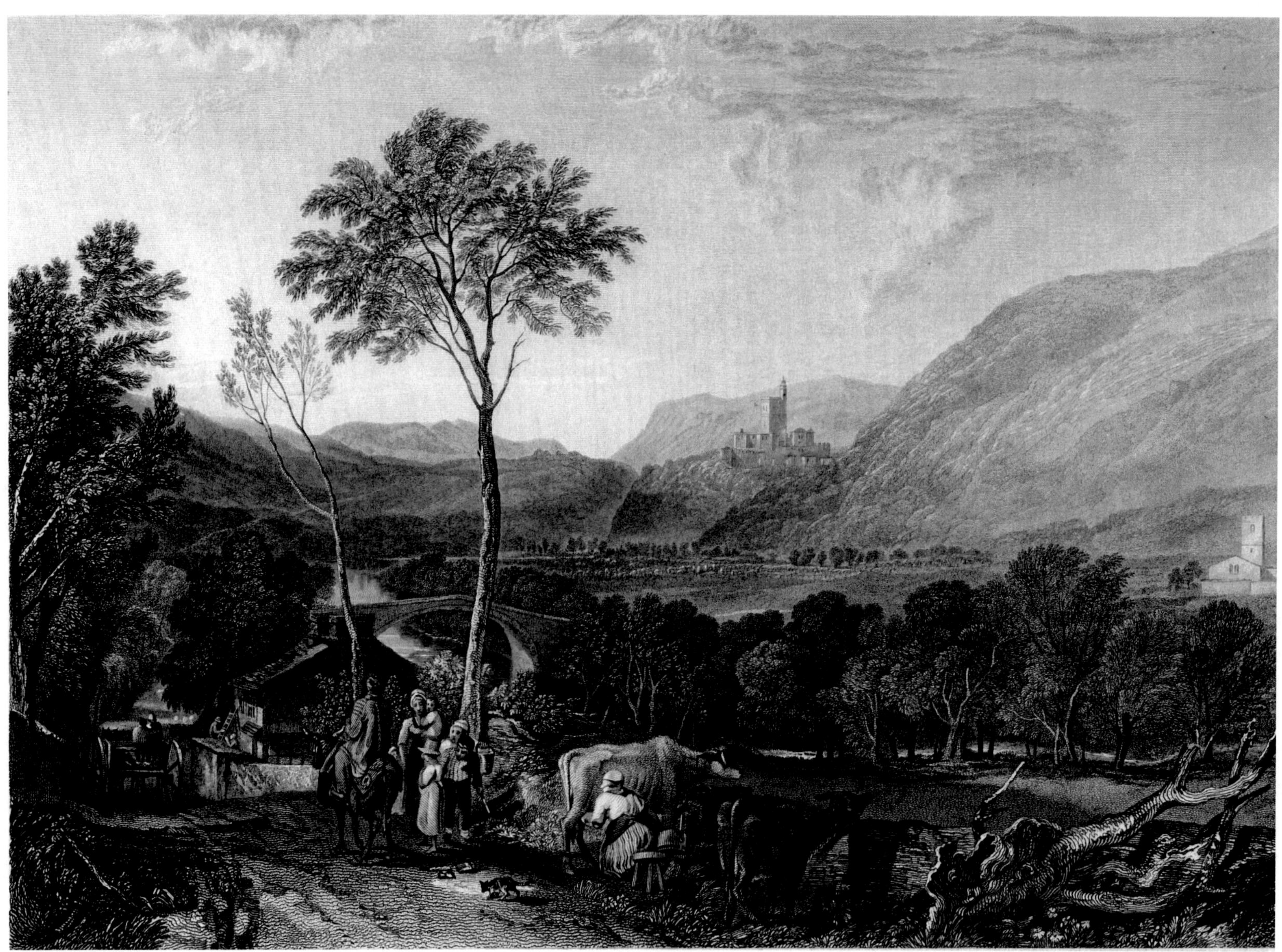

18: KIRKBY LONSDALE CHURCHYARD

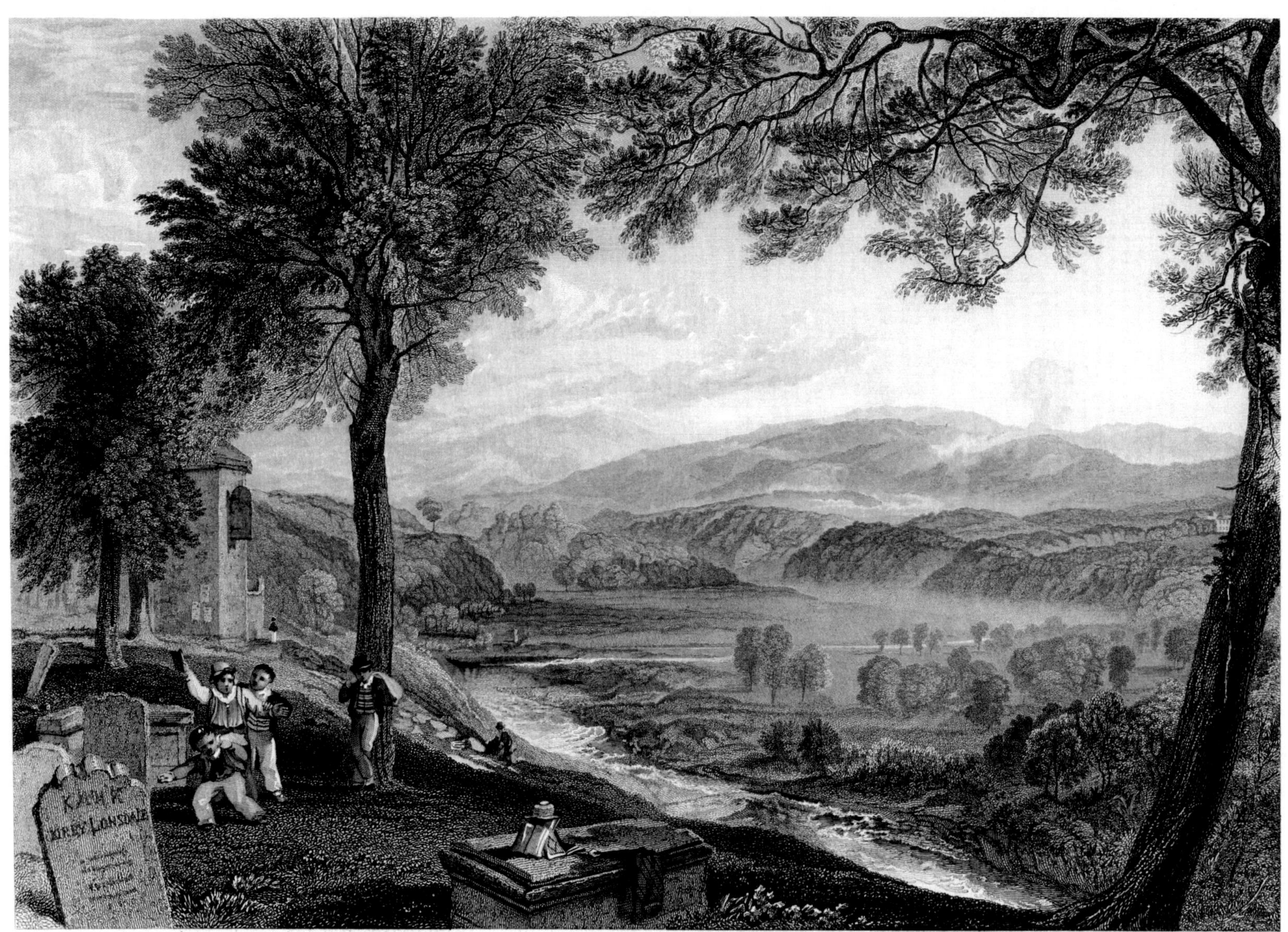
LONSDALE

19: HEYSHAM AND CUMBERLAND MOUNTAINS

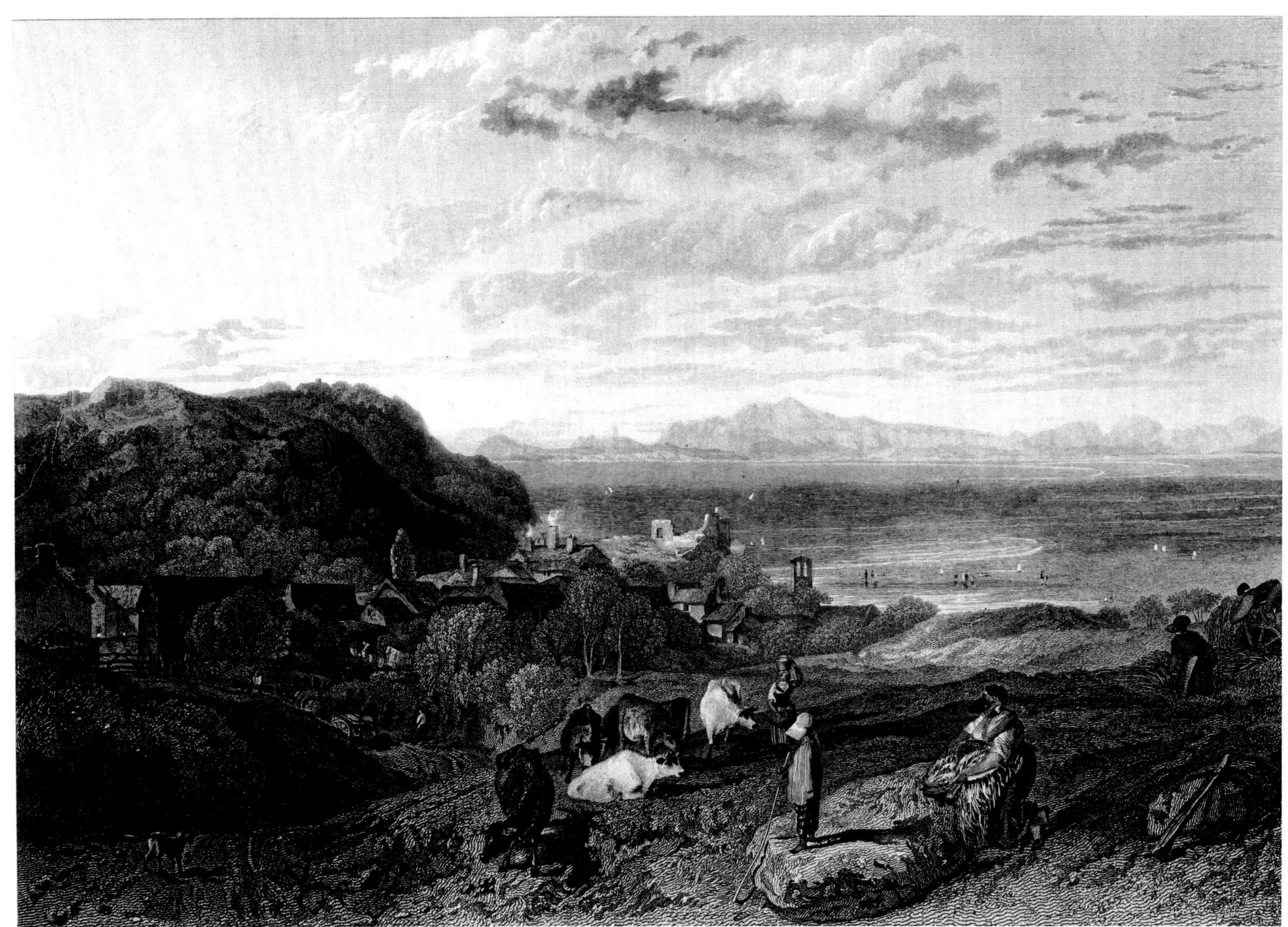

20: WEATHERCOTE CAVE WHEN HALF FILLED WITH WATER

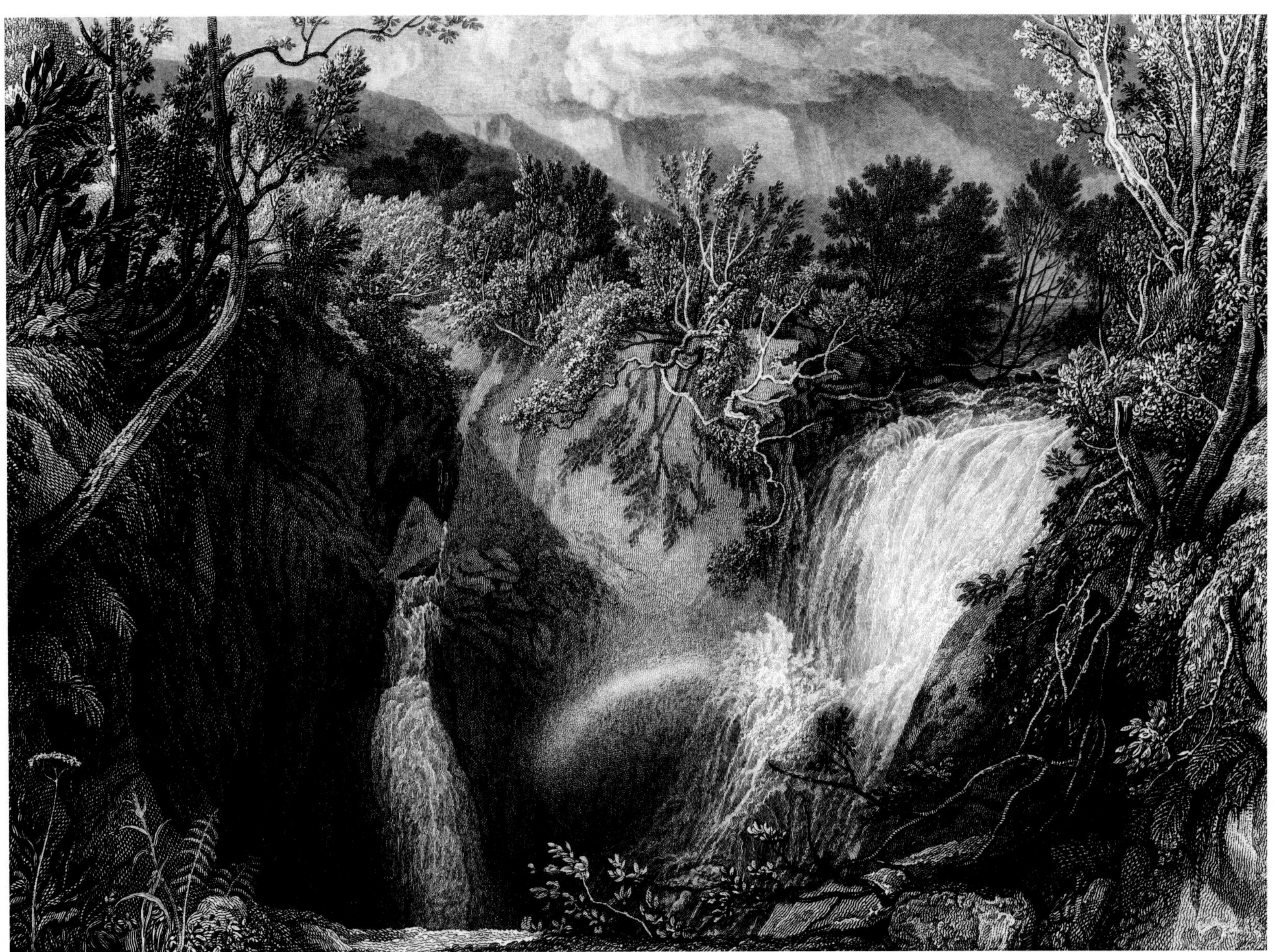

On 17 May 1816, the painter and diarist Joseph Farington met Turner at dinner and wrote: 'Turner told me he had made an engagement to make 120 drawings, views of various kinds in Yorkshire, – for which he was to have 3,000 guineas. Many of the subjects he required, he said, he had now in his possession. He proposed to set off very soon for Yorkshire to collect other subjects.' This enormous commission – the most valuable Turner ever received – was to illustrate a *General History of the County of York*, by the Revd. Thomas Dunham Whitaker, FRS, parish priest, antiquarian and prolific planter of trees.

Turner's journey round some of England's most inaccessible landscapes was hard: 'a most confounded fag', he wrote of travelling to Dufton, 'the passage out of Teesdale leaves everything behind for difficulty – bogged most completely Horse and its Rider, and nine hours making 11 miles.' In addition 1816 was 'the year without a summer', cold, with very poor light and incessant rain.

On his return to London Turner worked up the sketches and colour ideas into finished sketches from which specialist engravers would make copper plates for the printer. Unfortunately Whitaker died in 1821, and the publishers had overstretched themselves financially, so of the seven volumes originally planned only *An History of Richmondshire* was ever published, with just twenty of Turner's illustrations.